*Catholicism, Yoga
and Hinduism*

By
Franz Hartmann
C. Jinarajadasa

Copyright © 2020 Lamp of Trismegistus. All rights reserved. No part of this publication may be reproduced or transmitted in any form or by any means, electronic or mechanical, including photocopying, recording, or by any information storage and retrieval system, without permission in writing from Lamp of Trismegistus. Reviewers may quote brief passages.

ISBN: 978-1-63118-478-9

Esoteric Classics

Other Books in this Series and Related Titles

The Hymns of Hermes by G. R. S. Mead (978-1-63118-405-5)

Yoga, Hatha-Yoga and Raja-Yoga by Annie Besant (978-1-63118-476-5)

Buddhist Psalms by Shinran (978-1-63118-465-9)

Gnosis of the Mind by G. R. S. Mead (978-1-63118-408-6)

Clairvoyance and Psychic Abilities by A Besant &c (978-1-63118-403-1)

The Crest-Jewel of Wisdom by Adi Shankara (978-1-63118-475-8)

A Collection of Early Writings on Astral Travel (978-1-63118-477-2)

The Path of Light: A Manual of Maha-Yana Buddhism (978-1-63118-471-0)

The Golden Verses of Pythagoras: Five Translations (978-1-63118-479-6)

Tao Te Ching by Lao Tzu & Charles Johnston (978-1-63118-402-4)

The Book of the Watchers by Enoch (978-1-63118-416-1)

The Hymn of Jesus by G. R. S. Mead (978-1-63118-492-5)

Confessions of an English Opium-Eater by T De Quincey (978-1-63118-485-7)

Qabbalistic Teachings and the Tree of Life by M P Hall (978-1-63118-482-6)

Rosicrucian Rules, Secret Signs, Codes and Symbols by various (978-1-63118-488-8)

The Sepher Yetzirah and the Qabalah by M P Hall (978-1-63118-481-9)

History and Teachings of the Rosicrucians by W W Westcott &c (978-1-63118-487-1)

The Poem of Hashish by A Crowley & C Baudelaire (978-1-63118-484-0)

The Machinery of the Mind by Dion Fortune (978-1-63118-451-2)

The Star and the Garter by Aleister Crowley (978-1-63118-406-2)

The Leadbeater Reader: A Selection of Occult Essays (978-1-63118-483-3)

Audio versions are also available on Audible, Amazon and Apple

Table of Contents

Introduction...7

The Ritual Unity of Roman Catholicism and Hinduism
By C. Jinarajadasa...9

Yoga-Practice in the Roman Catholic Church
By Franz Hartmann...39

INTRODUCTION

The word "esoteric" can be difficult to define. Esotericism in general can be seen less as a system of beliefs and more as a category, which encompasses numerous, different systems of beliefs. It's a bit of juxtaposition, since the word "esoteric" indicates something that few people know about, while the term itself broadly covers numerous philosophies, practices, areas of study and belief systems.

In a greater sense, Esotericism acts as a storehouse for secret knowledge, which is often considered ancient (*by tradition, if not by fact*), passed down from generation to generation, in private. At various times in history, simply possessing the knowledge of some of these subjects, was considered illegal and a jailable offence, if discovered. This usually included such general topics as Alchemy, Pharmacology, Qabalah, Hermeticism, Occultism, Ceremonial Magic, Astrology, Divination, Rosicrucianism and so on. Collectively, these areas of study were often referred to as the esoteric sciences.

Sometimes, the outer garment of a subject isn't esoteric, while what is hidden beneath it, is. As an example, Freemasonry isn't necessarily esoteric by nature (at *least not anymore*), but certain signs, passwords and handshakes given to the candidate during their initiation, are in fact, esoteric, in the sense that they are hidden from the general public.

Today, in the twenty-first century, such topics are readily available at bookstores across the country, and numerous mainsteam publishers offer beginners guides and coffee-table volumes on many of these subjects, intended for mass appeal. Books like *"The Secret"* have turned previously arcane topics into household knowledge. All that being the case, however, it isn't to say that there still aren't buried secrets to uncover, ancient wisdom being ignored and forgotten mysteries to be explored. In fact, it is often that we are only able to further our own studies by standing on the shoulders of these disappearing giants.

Lamp of Trismegistus is doing its part to help preserve humanity's esoteric history by making some of these classics available to those students who are seeking to unearth the knowledge of these ancient colossi.

So, be sure to check other titles from our *Esoteric Classics* series, as well as our *Occult Fiction*, *Theosophical Classics*, *Foundations of Freemasonry Series*, *Supernatural Fiction*, *Paranormal Research Series*, *Studies in Buddhism* and our *Christian Apocrypha Series*. You can also download the audio versions of most of these titles from Amazon, Apple or Audible, for learning on the go.

THE RITUAL UNITY OF ROMAN CATHOLICISM AND HINDUISM

By C. Jinarajadasa

Two of the great religions today have as their fundamental theme the sacrifice of God for the sake of man. Hinduism clearly bases its sacrificial ritual on the sacrifice of Prajapati, the Lord of Creatures, who created the universe by a dismemberment of his Person. In Christianity the idea appears slightly changed, but in the dogma of the *Word made flesh*, the Son of God sent to be crucified as an Atonement for man, we have fundamentally the same mystic root.

Hindu ritual and that of the Roman Catholic Church have much in common, as both are intended to commemorate the sacrifice of the Deity. The Mass, as performed in the Roman Church, when studied in its occult aspects, leads us into deep mystic realms where we join hands on the one side with Hinduism, and on the other with Freemasonry.

Many, especially non-Roman Christians, little understand ritual and symbolism. They have an idea that ritual is so much mummery invented by priesthoods to hypnotize ignorant worshippers, and has no part in any true worship of God. When a Theosophist has trained himself to put aside religious bias, his knowledge that there are many paths to God puts him in an attitude of sympathy with a form of worship that satisfies millions today.

HIDDEN SIDE OF RITUALS

The mystic truth underlying true rituals is that what is done on earth is only symbolic of what is eternally taking place in the heavens. A rite as such has no efficacy unless it corresponds with some reality in the heavenly worlds. A ceremony to be of efficacy must be performed intelligently with a full understanding of the symbolism. When it is so performed, step by step a stately thought-form is built up in invisible matter, and this is utilized, sometimes directly by the Logos, and more often by Devas and others, to send to the celebrant and worshippers an outpouring of blessing and strength. Those even slightly sensitive will feel something of this outpouring in a heightened sense of spiritual things, and the few with clairvoyance of the invisible will see its tremendous nature.

THE WORSHIPER

Though a ritual is a common act of worship by a celebrant and congregation, yet it is only the priest that performs the mystery, and the worshipers have only an indirect part in it. The ceremony is done for them and they must follow with their thought what is taking place and help in the building of the invisible thought-form. Even if they do not intelligently follow each step, but yet believe heart and soul in the mystery at its culminating moment, that act of faith at-ones them with the outpouring from above.

THE CEREMONY OF THE MASS

The Mass, as performed in the Roman Church, has as its corner-stone the idea that God, as Jesus Christ, offers Himself a Victim and a Sacrifice to God in His undivided nature. The descent of the Son of God to be the Atonement is the one mystery in life, and there can be nothing more stupendous to contemplate daily. It is this sacrifice that is commemorated in the Mass, which is the sacrifice of the body and blood of Christ offered by Him to the Heavenly Father under the veils of bread and wine. Though the sacrifice on the cross was made in a *manifest and bloody manner,* the daily sacrifice on the altar is made in a mysterious and unbloody manner.

The ceremony crystallizes in a brief ritual, by means of symbolic acts, the life and ministry of Christ. Within the space of half an hour is symbolically enacted the whole life-history, and though the Mass, as a ritual, has been slowly built up, it is nevertheless one of the most splendid creations of the religious imagination. The culminating point of the life is the Last Supper and the Crucifixion, and the Mass enacts them over again.

THE CHURCH AND THE ALTAR

The church is dedicated to God and freed from any harmful magnetism by a long and elaborate ceremony of blessing and consecration. The nave is strewn with heaps of ashes on which with the end of the pastoral staff the consecrating bishop draws the letters of the Greek and Roman alphabets, and the walls are asperged with holy water.

The altar symbolically represents the table of the Last Supper. In a Roman church an altar is not such unless there be on it a stone slab consecrated by a bishop. Five crosses are hammered on the stone by him to represent the five wounds. Under it are placed relics of saints and other objects of good magnetism. The altar is covered with three cloths to represent the linen towels in which the body of the Lord was shrouded. The altar is covered throughout the year, except on Holy Thursday, when after Mass the altar is left bare, to symbolize the stripping of Christ's body and His abandonment during His passion.

THE PRIEST

It is the priest that offers the sacrifice for the people. He is an intermediary between man and God, and under divine sanction holds that position through ordination. He has a dual role, first as representing the people to God and offering up Christ to Him in their name, and then as Christ to the people. When the Mass is celebrated he wears the chasuble, that symbolizes the garment without seam torn from the Christ. On its front and back is a great cross, and as the priest celebrates Mass he is mystically the Christ bearing the cross. Except at High Mass, he has only an acolyte, representing the congregation, to serve him; but at High Mass he has assisting him the deacon, sub-deacon, and acolytes. Neither the deacon nor the sub-deacon, though they may be ordained priests, wear at Mass the chasuble with the cross.

THE VESTMENTS

Before coming to the altar the priest robes himself in the sacristy. He first covers his head and shoulders with the amice, saying, "Place upon my head, O Lord, the helmet of salvation, that I may be enabled to repel all the fiery darts of the wicked one," and then ties it round his waist. Then the alb, with, "Cleanse me, O Lord, and purify my soul, that, sprinkled with the blood of the Lamb, I may be fitted for the enjoyment of perfect felicity." With similar prayers he puts on the girdle of purity, on his left arm the maniple of sorrow and affliction, the stole symbolizing the robe of immortality forfeited by the first parents, and lastly the chasuble with the cross, saying, "O Lord, thou hast declared that thy yoke is sweet, and thy burden is light; grant that I may carry that which thou now dost impose upon my shoulders in such a manner as to merit thy grace."

THE RITUAL

The priest enters the church with a chalice and a paten on which is a wafer of bread, the ostia or host, *the victim* . With the sacrificial vessels are three cloths, (1) the corporal, so called because the Body rests upon it, (2) the pall or square covering of linen which is placed on the chalice, and (3) the purificatory to be used to wipe chalice and paten.

After placing the vessels on the altar, the priest descends to its foot, to represent man fallen and driven from Paradise, and arrived there signs-himself with the cross, saying, "In the name of the Father, * [*Wherever the asterisk is used in describing the ritual, there in the service the priest makes the sign of the cross*] the Son, and the Holy Ghost. Amen." Next he repeats, "I will go in to the altar of God, to God who rejoiceth my youth." This is followed by the 42nd Psalm. He then prays, confessing his sins of thought, word and deed, and after this gives the people absolution. Then follow extracts from the Psalms, and later two more prayers.

INTROIT AND KYRIE

Now begins the Introit or Entrance, and the prayer is read at the right or Epistle side of the altar from the Missal or Book. Next comes the Kyrie, "Lord, have mercy", thrice, to God the Father; three times to Christ, "Christ, have mercy"; and to the Holy Ghost three times, "Lord, have mercy." The Kyrie is a cry for mercy from fallen humanity. "Said before the Gloria", says a Catholic manual, "it expresses the profound misery of the world, and the immense need it had of redemption." The priest then goes to the middle of the altar, to represent the journey from Nazareth to Bethlehem, and recites the Gloria, the hymn the angels sang on Christmas eve. Here he kisses the altar to show he is united to Christ, the invisible High Priest, and turning to the people says, "The Lord be with you", and the response is given, "And with thy spirit." Seven times during Mass this salutation is given.

COLLECT AND EPISTLE

The celebrant says aloud, "Let us pray," but continues silently with the Collect, which is a prayer that collects the prayers of the faithful and is offered by the priest for them. Next comes the Epistle, and it consists of a reading from the letters of the Apostles or from the writings of the Prophets. As a part of the Mass it reminds the congregation of the Old Law. It is read with the face to the East, "because St. John the Baptist had always his eyes fixed upon the Messias, whom the Scriptures and the Church style the true Orient."

During the epistle the people remain seated, to figure the sad state of the old world, "them that sit in darkness and in the shadow of death." This is followed by a prayer called a Gradual or Tract, "the response of the faithful, the protestation of their good will and disposition."

THE GOSPEL

The book or Missal is now carried to the left or Gospel side of the altar. "This reminds us that when the Jews refused to listen to the teaching's of our Lord, the Apostles preached the true faith to the Gentiles in their stead." Before reading it the priest prays at the middle of the altar for purity of heart and lips. Then he makes the sign of the cross first upon the missal, then upon his forehead and mouth and breast, and the people cross themselves likewise. While the Gospel is being read the people listen standing, for it is no longer prophets and apostles that speak, but Christ Himself. During the reading the priest faces the north, for there the rebel angel has established himself, and it is only the Word of God that can bring to an end his domination.

After the Gospel ends the "Mass of the Catechumens." In the old church the converts who had not gone further and become *the faithful* were now dismissed, for their unprepared natures could not grasp the mystery about to be performed. "*Ite, missa est*", "Go, you are dismissed", was the phrase used, and from it the term missa or Mass has been derived.

CREED AND OFFERTORY

Now begins the repetition of the Nicene Creed, and at the words describing the Incarnation, "and was made man," all kneel in reverence of the mystery. This is followed by the Offertory, when the priest offers bread and wine, still merely bread and wine, to God. The paten with the host is elevated up to his breast, and looking up at the Crucifix he prays. Lowering he makes with it a sign of the cross and deposits it on the corporal on his right. Wine and water are mixed now in the chalice to symbolize how for our sakes God the Son put on our human nature, and the chalice is elevated to the level of the eyes and a prayer is said. It is lowered again with a sign of the cross and placed on the corporal and covered with the pall.

Next the priest offers the hearts of the faithful, and after recites the 25th Psalm, while washing the tips of his fingers in memory of Jesus washing the feet of His disciples. Returning to the middle of the altar, another prayer is said and offering is made to the Holy Trinity. Turning to the people, he says, "Brethren, pray that my sacrifice and yours may be acceptable to God the Father Almighty." The people respond, "May the Lord receive the sacrifice from thy hands, to the praise and glory of His name, and to our benefit, and that of His entire Holy Church." This is followed by a prayer called the Secret, the priest leaning forward, the hands joined in humiliation, to remind us how Jesus prayed in the Garden of Olives. Then aloud, priest and people, "World without end — Amen — The Lord be with you — And with thy spirit — Lift up your hearts

— We have lifted them up to the Lord — Let us give thanks to our Lord God — it is meet and just."

PREFACE AND SANCTUS

The Preface is the next prayer in the ritual. As the manual says, "We have entered into the way of the cross. Already the clamor of the multitude reaches us, the threatening of the tempest. Only a few hours now, and the Son of God will be bound, scourged, buffeted, put to death, and reckoned among the guilty". Next after the Preface comes the grand, "Holy, holy, holy, Lord God of Sabaoth. Heaven and earth are full of Thy glory. Hosanna in the highest. Blessed is he that cometh in the name of the Lord. Hosanna in the highest." And now in the invisible world round the altar the hosts of the cherubim and seraphim gather to watch and adore the sacred mystery.

CONSECRATION

The heart of the mystery now begins. It is called the Canon of the Mass. Kissing the altar to show his union with Christ, lifting his eyes and hands towards heaven, with the sign of the cross three times over the oblation, the celebrant prays, offering "these * gifts, these* presents, these* holy unspotted sacrifices"; then follows the commemoration of the living, praying silently for those he wishes to pray for. Here are invoked the Virgin Mary, various apostles, martyrs and saints. Then, spreading his hands over the bread and wine, he offers the oblation, "which oblation do Thou, O God, vouchsafe in all respects to bless,* approve,* ratify, and * accept; that it may be made for us the body* and blood* of Thy most beloved Son Jesus Christ our Lord. *Who the day before He suffered, took bread into His holy and venerable hands, and with His eyes uplifted towards heaven to Thee, the Almighty God, His Father, giving thanks to Thee, He blessed, brake, and gave it to His disciples, saying, Take and eat ye all of this. For this is My Body.*"

The priest kneels, adores, and elevates for all to see that the Lord is present. The server rings the bell, for of old a trumpet was sounded at the moment of crucifixion; and tradition says it happened for Christ's crucifixion, and the bell commemorates this. The priest continues, "In *like manner, after He had supped, taking alto this excellent Chalice with His holy and venerable hands, giving Thee also thanks, He blessed, and gave it to His disciples, saying, Take and drink ye all of this. For this is the chalice of My blood of the new and eternal testament, the Mystery of Faith, which shall be shed for you and for many, to the remission of sins. As often as ye do these things, ye shall do them in remembrance of Me."*

Kneeling, the celebrant adores the sacred Blood, and elevates for the congregation to see. Then he prays, "Wherefore, O Lord, we Thy servants, as also Thy holy people, calling to mind the blessed Passion of the same Christ, Thy Son, our Lord, His resurrection from the dead, and admirable ascension into heaven, offer unto Thy most excellent Majesty, of Thy gifts bestowed upon us, a *Victim, a holy *Victim, an unspotted *Victim, the holy *Bread of eternal life, and *Chalice of everlasting salvation. Upon which vouchsafe to look with a propitious and serene countenance, and to accept them, as Thou wast pleased to accept the gifts of Thy just servant Abel, and the sacrifice of our patriarch Abraham, and that which Thy high priest Melchisedec offered to Thee — a holy Sacrifice and unspotted Victim. We most humbly beseech Thee, Almighty God, command these things to be carried by the hands of Thy holy angels to Thy altar on high, in the sight of Thy divine Majesty, that as many as shall partake of the most sacred body* and blood* of Thy Son at this altar may be filled with heavenly grace and blessing, through the same Christ our Lord. Amen."

COMMEMORATION OF THE DEAD

The mystery of the Divine Outpouring affects all worlds, visible and invisible, of the living and the dead, and that the dead too may have part in it they are commemorated in the ritual. Then striking his breast to represent the repentance and confession of the thief on the right hand of Christ who acknowledged openly his guilt, the priest prays for fellowship with the apostles and martyrs for Himself and the people, "not in consideration of our merits, but of Thy own gratuitous pardon, through Christ our Lord. By Whom, O Lord, Thou dost always create, sanctify, quicken, bless, and give us all these good things. Through Him, and with Him, and in Him, is to Thee, God the Father Almighty, in the unity of the Holy Ghost, all honor and glory."

From the moment of consecration Christ is present with the people, not in any mystic fashion but as with the disciples in Palestine. Hence is now said the Lord's Prayer, which He Himself gave to the people. Using the words the Master gave, and with Him present, the people pray to God. It is only, perhaps, one who believes in the power of the Mass who can gauge the beauty and significance of this touching incident in the ritual.

The priest is now ready to *communicate* and breaks the Host from the right side into two parts, to commemorate the sacred wounds; and from one of the parts breaks a small piece which he puts into the chalice. As he puts the Host into the wine, he makes with it the sign of the cross on the chalice three times and says a prayer. The body and blood so joined symbolize the resurrection. Then he genuflects and strikes his breast, saying twice, "Lamb of God, who takest away the sins of the world, have mercy upon us." A third time he says it, but the last phrase is changed to *give us peace*.

Now follows a long prayer to Christ, and after it the celebrant takes the Host in his hands and says, "I will take the bread of heaven and call upon the name of the Lord." Three times now he strikes his breast and repeats those words full of faith of the Roman centurion, slightly changed at the end, "Lord, I am not worthy that thou shouldst enter under my roof; say but the word, and my soul shall be healed." Taking reverently both parts of the Host in his right hand, signing with it the cross on himself, he prays, "May the body of Our Lord Jesus Christ preserve my soul to everlasting life. Amen." Then he *receives* or *communicates*. Similarly he genuflects and adores and prays and communicates with the wine, and after, again prays, "May the blood of Our Lord Jesus Christ preserve my soul to everlasting life. Amen."

Lest any particles that remain in the chalice might be desecrated, he washes it twice and drinks the contents, with each ablution repeating an appropriate prayer. Then he turns to the book again and reads the Communion. Turning round, he blesses the people, and begins the last action of the ritual, a reading again from the Gospel. It is usually the Gospel of S. John, the first fourteen verses of the first chapter, priest and people kneeling at the words of the eternal mystery, "And the

Word was made flesh." The server responds, "Thanks be to God," and so the Mass ends.

THE OUTPOURING OF THE LOGOS

What is the real significance of the Mass? It is that of a wondrous outpouring. As the Host and Chalice are elevated and priest and people adore the Lord, the Logos sends down an outpouring and blessing. The particles of physical substance glow with His fire and there shines a radiant Star flashing to all sides. There to one at the far end of the church a Ray will shoot out, and here to another at the altar not one. It is only to such as are at one in utter belief of His presence, then, that He can send His quickening — a quickening that touches the man in his inmost nature, for a moment making his causal body to glow as a new-born star, for a moment waking that of a child-soul out of its dreaminess to the reality of the Life of the Logos around. To many a child-soul after death the only touch of the heaven world will be from this quickening at the Mass, for it may be no other activities of his life of passion will give him an ideal that will flower in heaven.

And as the Logos gives His outpouring to the worshipers, it is linked by Him to His beloved Son, Jesus, the Master of Christianity. Wherever He be, though a thousand times the Mass be performed each morning, Jesus knows and adds His blessing, too, to that of His Father.

Twenty centuries have passed and step by step the ritual of the Mass has been made by many hands. Yet behind it all was surely One guiding, so that a Form might be made for men on earth that He and the Heavenly Father could use. The Form is there today, in the Roman Church. Though in the book of the Karma of the world are written the many dark deeds of that Church against men, yet so long as it keeps the Sacrament of the Mass will it be a channel for God. It may well be, who knows, that that Church will yet change in outer and inner ways to be a real Holy Catholic Church proclaiming a life of the Spirit based on nature and a study of her laws. There may yet be on the throne of Peter not a man, but a god, even an Elder Brother of our humanity. May these things be, soon!

THE REAL PRESENCE IN RELIGIONS

It is not only in Roman Catholicism that one finds the idea of the presence of the Godhead during a certain part of the ritual. Wherever men gather for a common ritual, with a priest or a Worshipful Master, that element plays a leading part. In rituals in Egypt, Greece, and India, the presence of God or of a god appears prominently. As with the Mass, so too wherever a ritual has been built up, in Christianity, in Hinduism, or elsewhere, and men in their inmost hearts believe that God is present, and give Him their worship, He knows and responds, utilizing the form the worshipers give. The Real Presence is the heart and soul of a ritual, and in all true rituals He is there.

MASONRY

As we study rituals, it is instructive to note the parallel there is between the Roman ritual and that of Masonry. Certain signs and symbols are the same; the mark of the 33° Mason is that on the pastoral staff of an archbishop, and the cross and crown of the Knight Templar may be seen in almost any Roman church. As a ritual, that of Masonry is yet in the making, but knowing the history of rituals in India and Egypt, one can construct the lines of future development. Surely the mystic idea will be brought out that the Master who has been killed and comes to life again at the mystic word is the Archetypal Man; and as in Egypt the candidate at initiation was the Logos on the cross of matter, as the Roman priest with his chasuble at Mass is the Christ crucified, so too will the candidate be understood in the Masonic ritual of a future day. As at the Sanctus, cherubim and seraphim gather round, so too will it be known that in Lodge the denizens of the invisible love to take part with those in fleshly forms. And perhaps these two organizations, Masonry and Catholicism, that are so hostile today, will join hands recognizing a common work under the True Orient, when He comes again.

HINDU RITUALISM

In the beginning of the article it was mentioned that Hindu ritual and that of the Mass have much in common, as both symbolically depict God's sacrifice for man. In Christianity it is the Son of God that both offers Himself a Victim and is offered a Victim by church and people to God. Daily, before food and drink may pass his lips, the Roman priest must commemorate the sacrifice on Calvary.

THE SACRIFICE OF PRAJAPATI

In Hinduism the mystic idea of the Divine Sacrifice is as follows. Prajapati, "the Lord of Creatures," is the name for God in the sacrifice. "He is himself this very universe. He is whatever is, has been and shall be. He is the lord of immortality. All creatures are one-fourth of him, three-fourths are that which is immortal in the sky" (Purusha Sukta). But the universe became only because the Lord of Creatures offered Himself in sacrifice. "He toiled, He practiced austerity. Even as a smith, the Lord of Prayer together forged this universe; in earliest ages of the gods, from what was not arose what is." "By offering up his own self in sacrifice, Prajapati becomes dismembered; and all those separated limbs and faculties of his come to form the universe — all that exists, from the gods and Asuras (*the children of Prajapati*), down to the worm, the blade of grass, the smallest particle of inert matter. It requires a new, and ever new, sacrifice to build the dismembered Lord of Creatures up again, and restore him so as to enable him to offer himself up again and again, and renew the universe, and thus keep the uninterrupted revolution of time and matter."[*Shatapatha Brahmana,* translation in *Sacred Books of the East,* Vol. 43, Introduction, page xvii.]

PRAJAPATI AS VICTIM

If to the Christian the Cross of Calvary is a perpetual reminder of the great Sacrifice of the Son of Man, to be commemorated daily in the Mass, to the Hindu ritualist the Sacrifice of Prajapati must be commemorated daily in the sacrifice in the fire-altar. For "in this primeval" — or rather timeless, because ever proceeding — sacrifice, Time itself, in the shape of its unit the Year, is made to take its part, inasmuch as the three seasons, spring, summer and autumn, of which it consists, constitute the sacrificial oil, the offering fuel, and the oblation respectively. Prajapati .... the world man, or all-embracing Personality, is offered up anew in every sacrifice; and inasmuch as the very dismemberment of the Lord of Creatures, which took place at that archetypal sacrifice, was in itself the creation of the universe, so every sacrifice is also a repetition of that first creative act. Thus the periodical sacrifice is nothing else than the microcosmic representation of the ever-proceeding destruction and renewal of "all-cosmic life and matter".[ibid, page xv.]

THE FIRE ALTAR

In the West, it is the Son that offers Himself to the Father on the altar. Here in India it is the same. Agni, the son of Prajapati it is who restores his dismembered Father the Arch-Sacrificer. The great commemorative ceremony takes place not at an altar symbolic of the table of the Last Supper, but on a fire-altar in the shape of a bird flying to the east gate of heaven. During a whole year, laying a brick for each day, the altar is built. Seven layers are laid, to symbolize severally earth, air, sky, the sacrifice, the worshiper, the heavenly world and immortality. Four priests take part in the ceremony, the Adhvaryu who does the manual work, and two chanting priests, the Udgatr and the Hotr. The fourth priest is the Brahmana, or superintending priest, who takes no part physically in the ceremony, but performs the whole in his mind.

AGNI THE SON

At the bottom of the fire-altar is put a lotus leaf for the waters of space, from the womb of which son Agni and the human worshiper shall be born during the ceremony. For both are one, Agni the God and the mortal man. On the leaf is placed a gold plate symbolic of the Sun, which the worshiper has worn round his neck during the initiatory ceremony. On the Sun is laid a little gold man. This man is The Man, Purusha, in the Sun, the Logos. But He is, too, the worshiper, and it is the latter, through his image at the bottom of the altar, that shall rise at death through the three worlds of earth, air and sky to the realm of heaven.

On the last day but one of the year are sung the Great Chant and the Great Litany, whose verses are arranged to suggest the form of a bird. When the ceremony is over, Agni the Son has given up his body, the fire-altar, to build up anew his dismembered Father, to reconstruct the All. Though he has made the Many the One again, yet it is only in order that the Lord of Creatures might sacrifice Himself once again for our sakes, might once again crucify Himself on the cross of matter, that some day we may sit on His right hand "to judge the quick and the dead."

One further mystic truth comes in the ceremony in the identification of the Lord of Creatures with the human worshiper. As Prajapati is Lord of Time, so He is Lord, too, of Death. When the worshiper becomes one with Him through the sacrifice, he is one with death also. Death thenceforth ceases to have sway over him, for the Lord of Creatures, Life and Death, and man, are one.

THE ESSENCE OF ALL RITUALS

"Even as a grain of rice or the smallest granule of millet, so is the golden Purusha in the heart; even as a smokeless light it is greater than the sky, greater than the ether, greater than the earth, greater than all existing things; that Self of the spirit is my Self. On passing away from hence I shall obtain that Self. And, verily, whosoever has this trust, for him there is no uncertainty."

It is that trust in the truth, "I shall obtain that Self" that is ever given to men in Christian, Hindu, Masonic and other rituals, world without end.

YOGA-PRACTICE IN THE ROMAN CATHOLIC CHURCH

By Franz Hartmann

The study of comparative religion being one of the objects of the Theosophical Society, it may be of some interest to compare the yoga-practices of the Roman Catholic Church with those described in the Oriental writings. We will then find that they are to a certain extent identical, consisting principally in meditation (*prayer*), shakti, self-control, abnegation, faith, concentration, contemplation, etc, or what Shankaracharya describes as Shama, Dama, Uparati, Titiksha, Shraddha and Samadhana, not to forget bodily posture and the regulation of breath (*Pranayama*).

The most detailed instructions are contained in the writings of Ignatius de Loyola, a Catholic Saint, and founder of the (*later on ill-reputed*) Order of Jesuits. He was an officer in the Spanish army, born at Guipozcod in 1491, as the son of a nobleman. After having been severely wounded in battle, his mind took a religious turn; he abandoned his military career, became an ascetic, made a pilgrimage to Jerusalem, studied afterwards at Salamanca and Paris, and became in 1541 General of the Order of Jesuits. His writings have been translated into German by B. Kohler, and the following pages contain some extracts from the same.

The exercises prescribed by Loyola are calculated to develop the powers of the soul, especially imagination and will. The disciple has to concentrate his mind upon the accounts given in the Bible of the birth, suffering and death of Jesus of Nazareth, as if these were actual historical facts. He thus regards them, as it were, as a mental spectator, but by gradually working upon his imagination he becomes, so to say, a participator of it; his feelings and emotions are raised up to a state of higher vibrations; he becomes himself the actor in the play, experiences himself the joys and sufferings of Christ, as if he were the Christ Himself; and this identification with the Object of his imagination may be carried on to such an extent that even stigmata, or bleeding wounds corresponding to those on the body of the crucified Christ, will appear on his body. In this way compassion and love are awakened and developed within the soul, and as the love of a divine ideal is something quite independent of the correctness of the scientific opinion which we may have concerning the actual existence of that ideal itself, this way of awakening divine love by the power of imagination may be very well suited for those for whom love without an object is at first unattainable. Therefore the spiritual exercises of Loyola consist principally of regularly prescribed and gradually ordered meditations and contemplations of the passion of Christ. If properly executed, they may produce freedom from the illusion of self and awaken the power of discrimination (*Viveka*) between the eternal ego and the temporal self.

The exercises and penances, which Loyola taught to his disciples he practiced himself, and they were by no means easy.

He spent seven hours in prayer, and scourged himself three times every night for the purpose of subduing the desires of his *flesh*. Some of the Catholic Orders still practice such severe exercises. The Trappists, for instance, have to work very hard, and their only recreation is prayer. Each brother receives at his entrance to the Order a gown as his only garment, which he has to wear until the hour of his death, without ever being permitted to take it off, whether in daytime or at night, unless it should become so dilapidated as to have to be replaced by a more solid one. Their *Matins* begin at midnight, lasting for one hour, and one being followed at short intervals by others, so as to allow very little time for rest. They are exposed to the summer heat and have to do without fire in winter, being permitted only a hard bed to sleep on and barely sufficient cover. Moreover they are not permitted to speak with each other or with anybody, and the food they receive is hardly sufficient to keep up their strength.

The Catholic Church, as a whole, may be regarded an as *exoteric* school of religion, and the different Orders therein as *esoteric* schools for practicing Yoga. How far some of these Orders have become degraded and have lost the right to be called schools for Yoga, is not our purpose to investigate at present. Certain, however, it is that the Mysteries contained in the Catholic Church are far too high to be grasped by everybody, be he priest or layman, and that the greatest danger which threatens the Catholic Church is the great number of its followers who are incapable of understanding its true spirit, in consequence of which its doctrines are misrepresented and misunderstood. Nevertheless, in some of the Orders practicing the above-described austerities, some of these Mysteries are still alive. These people lead a life of great hardship, and there are probably only few among *our parlor-yogis* and would-be magicians willing to exchange places with them; but we meet smiling faces and joyous hearts among them, and the fact of their having voluntarily taken upon themselves *the Cross of Christ* testifies to their intrepidity and sincerity.

Loyola objects to theoretical explanations regarding the divine Mysteries, as they would only gratify scientific curiosity in unripe minds and disturb them; he only gives instructions concerning the practice of meditation, etc., because, if this practice is properly carried on, the Mysteries will reveal themselves in the natural course of time.

The states of mind under consideration are in their progressive order as follows:

1. *Cogitation.* The state in which the mind is moved and swayed by influences coming from without. These emotions have to be subdued.

2. *Concentration.* The ego assumes power over the thinking process, regulates his thoughts according to his will, and uses them accordingly.

3. *Meditation.* The ego closely examines the object upon which his mind is concentrated.

4. *Contemplation.* The mind enters the object of its meditation; it becomes an indweller of its sphere.

5. *Sanctification.* The mind becomes pervaded and sanctified by this association with the holy object; it becomes penetrated by its divine influence.

6. *Unification.* The contemplating mind becomes one with the object of its contemplation. To this may be added:

7. *Mortification.* Or the entire disappearance of the illusion of separateness; there is no separate self which knows, because the knower, the known and the knowledge are one.

The object of meditation is, as has already been stated, the life and suffering of Christ. This is divided into different periods for contemplation, from the Incarnation to the Crucifixion and Resurrection. At first only the memory is called into action by studying the supposed historical facts; next comes the imagination, associating itself with the actors in the divine play, and finally the mind becomes the actor itself; *i.e.,* Christ is born, lives, becomes crucified and resurrected within ourselves.

There are numerous instructions given as to how these practical exercises are to be carried out, of which we will mention the following:

The first thing is to free oneself from all sinful thoughts and sensual emotions, and to seek to realize the direct action of the divine will; one should not seek to pry with one's intellect into the divine Mysteries, but wait in humility for their interior revelation. This is far more useful in the end than lengthy explanations on the part of the teacher.

The disciple should, while engaged with one object of meditation during one week, not be informed of what will be the object given to him for the next period; but he should be warned against the aggressions of evil spirits, and have their nature explained to him.

He should meditate for five hours every day, beginning at midnight, each meditation lasting at least one hour, and he must not let his mind wander from the object of his meditation.

He should never make a solemn promise or vow until he is perfectly certain that he is able to keep it; that is to say, until God (*the Master*) Himself reveals to the soul His readiness to receive her. Then he does not follow his own selfish desires, but obeys the divine will.

The teacher should not seek to pry into the sins and innermost thoughts of the disciple; nevertheless he should observe him, so as to be able to give him such guidance and instruction as his case may require.

Ignorant and uneducated persons cannot be guided in the same manner as those who have more intelligence. No one should be offered spiritual truths, which he is not yet ripe enough to grasp or comprehend.

Each meditation should begin with prescribed prayers (the *Lord's Prayer, Ave Maria,* etc.).

The candidate should go to confession once in every week, and take every fourteen days the holy sacrament of communion.

He should separate himself from all his friends and acquaintances, and avoid all external disturbances, directing his mind solely to the service of God. The more he frees himself from all external attractions, the more will he become ready to receive the light, the grace, and the blessing of God.

The disciple should be instructed, according to the degree of his capacity to understand, about the origin and the real object of his life, which is to praise God and to serve Him. He ought to be made to see the relative worthlessness of all earthly things, and the value of that which is of eternal duration.

He should examine himself carefully every day, and compare the results of each examination with those of the previous one, in the same way as a father watches his child to see what progress it makes.

He should carefully avoid all doubt and despair and also all spiritual pride, and not dwell upon his own personal merits, but sacrifice them to God.

SPECIAL DIRECTIONS

Upon rising in the morning the disciple should at once firmly resolve to avoid all those sins of which he wishes to purify himself, and hold fast to that resolution during the day. Before retiring to rest he should examine himself again, to see whether he has been steadfast in his purpose, and it is useful to note his failures in some diary.

Resist and suppress every evil thought as soon as it arises. Avoid all useless talk and gossip.

Look upon all worldly possessions with contempt; desire nothing for yourself, neither bodily comfort nor mental consolation, neither riches nor fame.

The disciple should be indifferent to wealth or poverty, honor or disgrace, suffering and death, and always be ready joyfully to accept martyrdom for the glorification of Christ.

Here follow certain rules, which may be found somewhat objectionable from our point of view, namely:

He should never think of agreeable things, such as the joys of Paradise, but always have his mind dwelling upon grief and repentance for his sins, and think of death and the Last Judgment.

He should always keep his room dark and exclude all light, keeping doors and windows closed, except while he is praying, reading or eating.

He ought never to laugh, nor say aught that may cause hilarity in others. He ought never to look at anyone, except at receiving and taking leave of a visitor.

He ought to avoid in eating or sleeping not only that which is superfluous, but even as much as possible of what is considered necessary.

He ought to castigate and lacerate his body by means of lashes, applied with rods or ropes or in other ways, but without injuring the bones. This is for the purpose of doing penance for past sins and for conquering the lusts of the flesh, and also for entering into sympathy with the tortures suffered by our Lord Jesus Christ. [*It is hardly necessary to remark that these ascetic exercises have fallen generally out of use, and are only practiced by certain religious Orders at certain times, or by some especially fanatical persons*]

THE THREE METHODS OF PRAYER

The first method or step is to meditate successfully upon the seven mortal sins, the three powers of the soul, and the five senses of the body. This may be done while standing, sitting, kneeling, or in a recumbent position. While meditating upon the seven deadly sins, compare them with the seven cardinal virtues.

The second step is to meditate about the meaning of each separate word of the prayer, sitting or kneeling, and keeping the eyes either closed or gazing steadfastly upon some selected spot, and not letting his thoughts or eyes wander around. [Compare *Bhagavad-Gîta* VI, 13]

Thus he ought to remain for one hour or more, always beginning his meditation with an invocation, and ending with repeating the *Lord's Prayer, Credo, Anima-Christi* and *Salve Regina*. He ought not to proceed to meditate about another word before he has found in the previous one full satisfaction.

The third method consists in regulating the breath according to a certain measure of time. While drawing each breath some word of the prayer ought to be spoken within the heart, so that between each inhalation and exhalation, and during the whole time that this lasts, only one word is inwardly spoken. For instance, if you meditate about the *Lord's Prayer,* beginning with "Our Father, which art in heaven," let your whole attention be directed only to the word *our* and its meaning, and then proceed to the next word, etc.

THE MYSTERIES OF THE LIFE OF OUR LORD JESUS CHRIST

These Mysteries cannot be satisfactorily explained to the human intellect; but they can be spiritually grasped by identifying oneself with the events historically described in the *New Testament,* and mentally participating therein.

In this way the imagination acts upon the will and the emotional nature, causing the higher vibrations of the soul to enter into action, to lift the mind up to the region of spiritual perception, and the love of God to enter the heart. It is then necessary to learn to discern between good and evil influence. Only God has the power to illuminate the mind without any preceding cause; but if there is such a cause, the good angels, as well as the evil ones, may send comfort to the soul; the first ones with good intentions, the evil ones with an evil object (*such as to incite vanity or spiritual pride, etc.*) in view, and the evil spirit may assume the shape of a messenger of light for the purpose of leading us to perdition. We therefore ought to examine the origin, current, and object of our thoughts. If the beginning, the middle and the end are good and the object the highest, it is the sign of a good influence; but if the thoughts are disturbed by doubts and turned to inferior objects, it is a sign that an evil spirit is at their back. Moreover the touch of a good influence is mild and sweet, and that of an evil one at first harsh and disturbing; but if the heart is inclined to evil, the evil spirit also enters silently, as if it were into his own house through the open door.

Finally it may be of some interest to hear what Loyola says in regard to the Church:

We must never use any judgment of our own, but be always ready to obey in all things the orders of the true bride of Christ, our holy mother, the Church.

If I see that a thing is white and the Church calls it black, I have to believe in its being black.

We must always approve of and praise the sayings and doings and manners of our superiors, whatever they may be; even if they are not such as can be praised publicly, because to do so would lower these persons in the estimation of the crowd.

One ought not, to the ignorant, to say much about *predestination* (*Karma*); because, instead of working for their own improvement, they will become lazy and say: "Why should I trouble myself? — If it is my predestination to be saved, I will be all right, and if I am predestined to be damned, I cannot prevent my damnation." One ought also not to speak about the divine grace of God as if it were a gift, rendering all our own works unnecessary. The highest truths are frequently misunderstood, and the best medicine becomes a poison if misapplied.

Some of the rules given by S. Ignatius de Loyola may be objectionable, but nowhere do we find among them the often quoted Jesuitical maxim that the object sanctifies the means. Moreover there is no doubt that while an object, be it holy or unholy, cannot sanctify its means, a holy purpose can and will sanctify the means, provided they are neither holy nor unholy, but indifferent. Thus for instance, the using of a knife upon a man's body may be a holy or unholy act. If it is done for the purpose of cutting his throat, it is unholy; but if the surgeon uses it for saving a person's life it is holy, and the purpose sanctifies the means.

The Roman Catholic Church has originally derived its doctrines and practices, and even its ceremonies, from the Northern Buddhistic School. Loyola is a true representative of its spirit. His spiritual exercises are in many ways identical with the instructions given in the East for the practice of Raja-Yoga, and a comparison of the two systems may be useful for those who do not merely desire to gratify their curiosity in regard to the astral plane, but desire to become more spiritual by letting the divine powers within their soul become awakened and developed through the influence of divine Love, divine Wisdom, and eternal Life.

www.ingramcontent.com/pod-product-compliance
Lightning Source LLC
LaVergne TN
LVHW041500070426
835507LV00009B/725